Lake Life

Memories Journal

MEMORIES MADE AT THE LAKE LAST A LIFETIME

Made in the USA
Monee, IL
07 April 2023

31509229R00068